PARENTING CHIL.

This handbook is intended to be used in conjunction with the Family Time course *Parenting Children*. A handbook should be provided for each participant on the course.

More information on courses, delegate materials, downloadable speakers' resources, invitations and posters is available via the Family Time website *www.family-time.co.uk*, or phone Family Time on 020 8799 3778.

Parenting Children

Course Handbook

MARK AND LINDSAY MELLUISH

KINGSWAY PUBLICATIONS
EASTBOURNE

First published 1999 as *Family Time Handbook*
Substantially revised new edition 2007

Bible quotations are from the New International
Version © 1973, 1978, 1984 by the International Bible Society.

Cover design by Pinnacle Creative (www.pinnaclecreative.co.uk)

ISBN 978 184291 356 7

KINGSWAY COMMUNICATIONS LTD
Lottbridge Drove, Eastbourne BN23 6NT, England.
Email: books@kingsway.co.uk

Printed in Great Britain

Contents

1
A Vision for the Family

What has happened to parenting?

It used to be that parenting skills were passed down, mistakes were learned and new discoveries were shared. This does not happen so much any more because of the ways in which our communities have changed.

Leading the family

'Family' will mean something different to each person. For some it will mean a mum and dad and their children; for some it will be a mum or dad parenting the children alone; for others it may mean a mum and dad with children and grandparents or an aunt or uncle; for others still it may mean a mum with her children coming together with a dad and his children.

Have a vision and work towards it

'What's family life going to be like and how is it going to work out?'

1. Family values

That end destination will shape the *values* that we have in our family and those values will shape the way in which we work as a family in the here and now. They will give our family its individual feel, its DNA.

The story of the lost son (Luke chapter 15) tells of a son who went off, probably in his teenage years, and spent his father's inheritance getting into all sorts of trouble, but there was something inside of him that still wanted home. When he was in trouble it was home that he went to because he knew that the value of forgiveness was there. He knew his father would take him back. If he hadn't known that value he wouldn't have returned.

- What is my family like now?
- What is my vision or dream for my family?

Dream dreams for your family

Take a few moments to think about your hopes and dreams for your family. Write down your top three dreams for your children's lives:

1.

2.

3.

How long does it take for dreams to come true?

It helps to have the long term in mind.

Nothing worth having comes easily

We may have resorted to one of the following:

- *An authoritarian approach* – 'Do as I say not as I do'.
- *A permissive approach* – 'I'm worn out with it all so I'll ignore what they're doing and hope they soon grow out of it'.

- *Bribery* – 'Clean your room and I'll treat you to an ice-cream'.
- *Emotionalism* – ' I won't love you if you do that'.
- *A punishment-driven approach* – 'If you don't stop that I'll . . .' i.e. control through threat of punishment, rather than punishment being used as a corrective measure.

2. The heart

It's from our hearts that we are motivated to do things

'Above all else, guard your heart, for it is the wellspring of life' (Proverbs 4:23).

If we can reach our children's hearts with healthy values, then ultimately we will see those same values worked out in their lives.

3. A firm foundation

Why use the Bible?

The Bible touches every area of life in some way.

4. Our example

Children may not be very good at listening to their elders, but they nearly always seem to find ways of imitating them
---

We reproduce who we are not what we say.

**It is unreasonable to expect a child to listen to
your advice and ignore your example**

Taking it further

1. Think about the hopes and dreams that you have for your family at this stage.
2. Try to provide the reason 'why' when you ask your child to do something (if you don't do this already), and note the response.
3. Try to consider the circumstances before making parenting decisions this week.
4. Review the example that you set for your children now, or if your children are very young (or have not arrived yet) think about the example you hope to set in the future.
5. Read Chapter 1 of *Parenting Children*.

2
Love and Marriage

The family is the primary social unit of our society and it is one worth protecting and keeping. For family relationships to grow, families need to spend time together.

1. Mum and Dad's relationship

The most important thing a father can do for his children is to love their mother

---

If you are married and living with your partner. . .

- even though you have children, your relationship with your partner is the most important relationship in the family
- the quality of all the relationships in the family and also the security of our children will depend on the quality of the mum and dad's relationship

Life often is very hard and challenging for those who are bringing up children without the support of a partner.

What if you are parenting on your own?

As you parent alone, your special significant relationships with friends and family members will be important for you.

If you have a relationship with God and are relying on him to help you raise the family, that will also be a source of support and strength, as it will be for those who are married.

2. The relationship of the children within the family

To live our lives centred around the children may be detrimental to family life.

If a child learns that he is at the centre of the family he may become self-centred. He may be a taker and not a giver.

If he sees himself as a member of a team, he will be confident and secure, making relationships naturally and comfortably, giving and receiving, knowing the importance of investing in relationships.

Keep a healthy perspective on all your relationships. If you are married keep that relationship as a priority.

3. How can I learn to say 'I love you' in all these relationships?

'Over all these virtues put on love' (Colossians 3:14).

Accounts for love

Each of us has a love bank with an account for each and every person we know.

The love languages

- Words of affirmation
- Quality time

- Gifts
- Acts of service
- Physical touch

Our children and their love languages

When children are little it is difficult to know what is their primary love language, so pour on all five and you are bound to be right! If you watch them you can discover it early.

How can you discover your own primary love language?

Ask yourself these questions:

- What makes me feel most loved by my partner or close family member, friend or child? What do I desire above all else?
- What does my partner or child or friend do or say that hurts me? If criticism springs to mind, maybe yours is words of affirmation.
- What have I most requested of my partner? The thing you most request is probably the thing that would most make you feel loved.
- How do I most express love to other people? Often we express love in the way we would like it expressed to us.

Take time now to do the exercise below using it to work out your primary love language and to work out the order of the other four. Then try to work out the order for your partner and your children.

LOVE LANGUAGES EXERCISE

My love languages are:

1.

2.

3.

4.

5.

My partner's love languages are:

1.

2.

3.

4.

5.

My children's love languages are:

1.	1.	1.
2.	2.	2.
3.	3.	3.
4.	4.	4.
5.	5.	5.

Taking it further

1. Consider this question: does your family life revolve chiefly around your children or are the needs of each member of the family considered to be equally important?
2. This week, when you come home in the evening, try spending five minutes talking with your husband or wife before taking time with the children. See how your children respond.
3. Read Chapter 2 of *Parenting Children.*

Recommended reading for this session

Gary Chapman, *The Five Love Languages*, Northfield Publishing, 1995.
John and Anne Coles, *Making More of Marriage,* New Wine International, 2000.
Willard F. Harley, *His Needs, Her Needs*, Fleming H. Revell Co., 1995.
Nicky and Sila Lee, *The Marriage Book*, HTB Publications London, 2000.
Rob Parsons, *Loving Against the Odds*, Hodder & Stoughton, 1998.

3
When They Are Young

If we hope to shape our children in such a way that they take on board for themselves the things we teach them, then it is vital that:

- our relationships with them are strong
- channels of communication are always open
- our children know we love them

How can we reach our goal?

1. Time

Presence is spelt T-I-M-E

Children need our time today and it is not just quality time they need but quantity time.

A key to communicating with children is to put in a lot of quantity time so that the quality time can happen.

The best thing parents can spend on children is time, not money
---

EXERCISE: TIME SPENT WITH MY CHILDREN

Take a few moments now to discuss the chart below with your partner or neighbour, and use it to review the time you spend with your children.

1. Write down in the first column the amount of time per session that you are available to your children this week.
2. Write down in the second column the amount of time you are able to give them your full attention.

	Weekday Time Available	Weekday Full Attention	Saturday Time Available	Saturday Full Attention	Sunday Time Available	Sunday Full Attention
Morning						
Early Afternoon						
Late Afternoon						
Evening						
Total this week:						

2. Communication

What can we do to encourage communication when we are with our children?

Practical tips

- Physically get down to the level of your child. Perhaps kneel or sit when they are talking.
- Look them in the eye. Show them that they have your full attention.

- Don't try and do two things at once – listen only to your child.
- Reassure them that they have your attention by touching them on the face or arm.
- Wait for them to finish what they are saying! It may take a while but it is worth it.

Three worlds

- Our public world, the part of us that is open for anyone to see.
- Our personal world, which is open to those close to us.
- Our private world, which we open up just every now and then to those we trust.

Allow your children into your world too.

3. Building relationships

a) Do things together.
b) Encourage with words.

> 'Encourage one another and build each other up' (1 Thessalonians 5:11). The word *encourage* means 'to instil courage'. In giving a child encouragement we are looking to give him the courage to go further, to enlarge his borders.

c) Give plenty of hugs.
d) Keep your promises.
e) Tell your children regularly that you love them.

A word to dads . . .

Dads have an equally crucial role to play in family life as mums, providing a role model for their boys and affirming femininity for their girls.

Build relationship with your children while you have the chance.

As we spend time with our children now, building a relationship of trust, we are laying the foundations for a life of unity in the family.

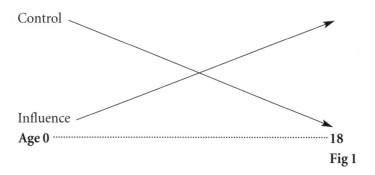

Fig 1

Taking it further

1. Begin to work on listening and communicating in the ways this session has suggested, and see how your child responds.
2. Try to be aware this week of how good you are at listening to your partner or to other adults.
3. Look for opportunities to encourage and praise your children.
4. Read Chapter 3 of *Parenting Children*.

Recommended reading for this session

Gary Chapman and Ross Campbell, *The Five Love Languages for Children*, Northfield Publishing, 1995.

Adele Faber and Elaine Maglish, *How to Talk so Kids Will Listen and Listen so Kids Will Talk*, Avon Books, 2002.

Rob Parsons, *The Sixty-Minute Father*, Hodder & Stoughton, 1995.

4
Family Time

The people our children become are products of two things:

- their life experience
- how they interact with that experience

When children are young the family is one of the major influences on them. Many aspects of family life have a bearing on who our children become.

1. Our family make-up

- Family structure
- Family roles
- Family conflict
- Family failure
- Family history
- Family values

It is never an indication of failure to see a need to make changes in family life.

EXERCISE: FAMILY PATTERNS

Circle your responses to the following points, then talk with your partner or your neighbour about your experiences.

In my childhood home . . .

We used to make jokes often/sometimes/rarely.

We used to touch each other frequently/sometimes/hardly ever.

Kisses and cuddles were normal/measured/rare.

When people felt angry they hit out/rowed/sulked/talked.

We would discuss our plans fully/partly/reluctantly.

My business was everybody's/interesting/my own.

We prided ourselves on our concern/interest/independence.

Nakedness was accepted/avoided/frowned upon.

Sex was discussed/readily/when necessary/never.

Children were disciplined by Dad/by Mum/by both/by neither.

Children said prayers with my dad/my mum/both/neither.

We went out together/independently/rarely.

I liked it when my dad . . .

I liked it when my mum . . .

I was happy when . . .

Today in my immediate family . . .

What my child might say they like best about my family is . . .

What I like best about my family is . . .

I can rely on my family to . . .

Something my parents did that I do not want to happen in my home is . . .

I expect to be in touch with my relatives daily/weekly/monthly/two or three times a year/as little as possible.

2. Family identity

If family identity is strong, if our children feel involved in and proud to belong to their family, they are more likely to hold to its values and principles.

How can we build a strong family identity?

a) Be a team

Being a team means supporting and encouraging the team members

---

b) Have a set Family Time

- A time to discuss
- A time to teach
- A time to prepare
- A time to laugh together
- A time to pray together

c) Family jobs

- Set the table for a meal
- Feed pets
- Make drinks
- Make beds in the morning
- Help with cleaning
- Tidy garden of toys
- Make cups of tea or coffee
- Clear up toys
- Put dirty clothes in the wash basket
- Clean windows
- Wash car
- Help with washing up
- Help with ironing
- Cook a meal

d) Family quote book

e) Family photos

f) Family traditions

g) Be together

Families who spend significant amounts of time together as a unit are more likely to turn out confident children

---

Meal times
Hi-low
Do things together . . .

- Go for cycle rides

- Have a family pizza night with a good video
- Go for walks together
- Eat meals together as often as possible
- Sleep in the tent together in the garden
- Sit in church together
- Eat ice-creams together
- Do the gardening together
- Read a book together
- Make family holidays a priority

Taking it further

1. Consider the structure of your family and what effect it might have on your child or children. Are there things that you would like to change and can change?
2. Consider steps you might take to strengthen the identity of your family.
3. Try having a Family Time and see how your children respond.
4. Read Chapter 4 of *Parenting Children*.

5

Outside Influences

As our children grow older and begin to have the freedom to be a bit more independent, outside influences become stronger and they are going to be faced not only with positive ideas and activities but with negative ones as well. We as parents can be aware of these influences, and try to prepare our children for this and equip them to make decisions based on what is right and good.

1. External influences on our children

Television

- The average father spends three minutes a day in 'quality' conversation with his children.
- The average mother spends five and a half minutes in 'quality' conversation with her children.
- One in three children under the age of six watches television for between two and six hours a day.
- A third of children under three have a television set in their bedroom.

Computer

School

Friends

Other adults

Significant others

Extended family

EXERCISE: EXTERNAL INFLUENCES

Look at this list and using the diagram below note down how many hours each week your children spend with this person or doing this activity. Then ask yourself how helpful or not that person or activity is. Try to be as specific as possible.

Ask yourself the following questions:

- Who has the greatest influence on my children?
- Am I happy about this influence?
- Does anything need changing?
- Who else is helping me bring up my children?

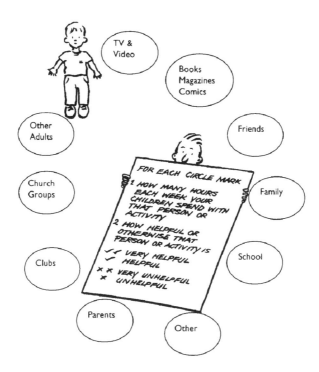

2. Our children's relationship with God

Our children respond to their surroundings, to the influences around them, according to where their hearts are.

> **Children are not just passive receivers of outside influences. They are active responders**

As our children interact with their childhood experience, their response will be affected by:

- whether they have good relationships within the family, where opinions and problems can be raised and discussed

- whether they are aware of the values of the family and to what extent they have taken on those values (more on this next session)
- whether they have good relationships with other trusted adults to whom they can go and discuss things
- whether they have good friendships with peers who encourage them to fulfil their potential
- whether they have been taught to question and think things through for themselves
- their perception of God

How can we encourage our children in their relationship with God?

a) Pray for them.

b) Pray with them.

c) Be open with them about your own faith.

d) Let them see you reading your Bible and praying.

e) Go together as a family to church.

f) Encourage them to enjoy the Bible themselves.

Taking it further

1. Review the list of influences on your children and think about any changes you may want to make.
2. Consider your child's relationship with God. Look at how you might encourage him or her to develop that relationship.
3. Read Chapter 5 of *Parenting Children*.

Recommended reading for this session

Stormie Omartian, *The Power of a Praying Parent*, Kingsway Publications, 1996.

Various children's books and Bibles.

6
Transmitting Values

Our aim as parents is to bring up children whose lives are an outward expression of a right heart

---

1. Our family values

a) What is a priority and what isn't?
b) What causes Mum and Dad to 'get cross' and what goes by without them even commenting?
c) What value do we place on material possessions?
d) How important are friendships and family relationships?
e) Is keeping the house tidy too important to allow friends home for pizza and Coke, or are people welcome in our home at any time?
f) What attitudes do the children grow up with?
g) Is a relationship with God central to family life, or does life go on from week to week without reference to him?

• What values did you grow up with in your family?

• What values do you have now?

Look at the list of values below and see whether or not you agree with the statements.

- God is number one in our lives. We should make time to worship him and not speak in a way that is dishonouring to him.
- Family relationships are important, especially the ones between parents and children.
- It is wrong to take another person's life.
- Marriage is a God-given thing and is the right place for sex.
- We should always pay for what we want to own unless we are given it as a gift. Taking something that belongs to someone else is wrong.
- Honesty and truth are needed for the smooth running of society. It is wrong to tell lies, as is the dishonesty of putting someone else in a bad light.
- It is wrong to be jealous of what other people have and think that you should have it as well. People are more important than possessions. Other people matter.
- We should respect the law and those in authority.

(Based on the Ten Commandments – Exodus 20:1–17)

Take a few minutes now to discuss these values and the questions above them with your partner or neighbour and see if you can work out your top five most important values for you and your family.

1.

2.

3.

4.

5.

2. How can these values provide a framework for our children's lives?

We want to place into their hearts values that are good and honest.

The conscience

It's out of our 'heart' or 'conscience', our understanding of what is right and wrong, that our attitudes and values come.

Psalm 119:11 says 'I have hidden your word in my heart that I might not sin against you.' David, the writer of that psalm, had hidden God's direction for life in his own heart and we can, in the same way, 'hide' or 'place' good values in our children's hearts.

The value library

The heart is the area in which are placed and stored values or principles for life. It's a bit like a 'value library', a framework with empty shelves waiting to be filled.

Value search system

For each new situation we meet, a search system comes into play, scanning the shelves of the value library, our conscience, for the corresponding value.

Honesty

Honesty is powerful in building strong, healthy relationships within the family.

Dishonesty comes through . . .

• not telling the truth:

    – Consider the age of your child
    – Consider the motive behind the lie
    – Consider your child's general level of honesty

• taking things that belong to someone else:

    – Consider the seriousness of what has happened
    – Consider the context

3. How do we input these family values?

In their very early years we will be directing our children by using quite a few negatives. So we find ourselves saying 'No' or 'Don't touch' several times a day. At this stage our parenting will involve lots of restrictions, warnings and consequences.

From around the age of three, we can change the approach from a negative to a much more positive form of shaping – one in which our child begins to understand the reasons behind what we are asking of them.

Here are three practical ways of inputting positively into their hearts. We can

a) provide the reason 'why' when we ask them to do or stop doing something
b) answer their questions in such a way as to teach the values that are important to us

c)   ask them questions to enable helpful discussion to follow

Encouraging a healthy conscience

- *A healthy conscience* is marked by an attitude of 'I'll do this because it is right', motivated by choosing to do the right thing.
- *An unhealthy conscience* is marked by an attitude of 'I must do this or else I'll be punished'.

A healthy conscience can more easily develop if. . .

a)   a child knows Mum and Dad love him unconditionally, rather than their love depending on his good behaviour
b)   Mum or Dad can try to respond to bad behaviour by correcting it and moving on rather than looking to make the child feel guilty
c)   Mum or Dad can seek to input strong values and explain the reason for upholding them

- What values are we placing in our children's hearts?
- How are we placing them?
- Are we aware of living out and encouraging in our children healthy values, emphasising that other people matter?

THE HEALTHY CONSCIENCE TEST

Try doing this test on yourself to see what sort of conscience you have. Give yourself a score for each statement, according to the scale given below.

Scale: 1 = Never true of me
         3 = Sometimes true of me
         5 = Half yes/half no

7 = Usually true of me

10 = Always true of me

1. I am uncomfortable in a discussion where my view or opinion is different from that of the other person.
2. I find it hard to say 'no' when someone makes a request of me which would add to an already over-busy schedule.
3. When a friend is distant or preoccupied I tend to assume it's because of something I've done wrong.
4. I often end up doing something I don't really want to do for fear that if I don't, people will criticise me in my absence.
5. When someone says they want a meeting with me next week but don't say what about, I spend a lot of time worrying that I have done something wrong.
6. I often find myself offering to do things for people out of guilt rather than a genuine desire to help them.
7. I am easily unsettled if my parents-in-law don't agree with the way I discipline my child(ren).
8. I am afraid to discipline my child(ren) for fear that they won't love me any more.
9. I feel guilty when I cannot comply with what my mother or father is asking of me.
10. I pay more attention to the criticism of one person than to the praise and admiration of the other ninety-nine.
11. I constantly look for affirmation from those closest to me.
12. I often find myself quickly apologising in order to make peace, even though I don't feel I am to blame.

For an analysis of total scores see Notes at end of handbook.

Taking it further

1. Look for opportunities to explain the reason 'why' when children ask questions about everyday life.
2. Try to be aware of your own responses to situations and ask yourself why you do what you do.
3. Read Chapter 6 of *Parenting Children*.

Recommended reading for this session

J. John, *Ten*, Kingsway Publications, 2000.

7
Guiding and Shaping

Real discipline is to do with reaching and shaping the hearts of our children.

'Listen, my son, and be wise, and keep your heart on the right path'(Proverbs 23:19).

Our job as parents is to instruct and guide our children to encourage them to have hearts that are wise.

1. What are the benefits of children doing as Mum or Dad asks?

For children to do as parents ask:

- brings safety for our children
- will help them in their own relationship with God
- helps them to respond well to authority

  – authority is needed for order
  – authority helps us to be considerate and think of others

If we respect authority our children are more likely to do the same.

2. How do we get there?

Sometimes as parents we undermine our own efforts to have our children carry out our requests:

- We threaten and we repeat ourselves.
- We use bribes.
- We negotiate in the midst of conflict.
- We misuse compassion.
- We offer too much choice.

Here are ten tips to help our children towards doing as we ask

1. Say what you mean and mean what you say.
2. Be careful how you phrase your instruction.
3. Get eye contact and a verbal response.
4. Don't be too quick to repeat yourself.
5. Expect a response.
6. Provide a warning.
7. Offer a door of escape.
8. Consider the setting.
9. Be consistent.
10. Remember your example.

Conflict is inevitable in every family and it is helpful to see it not as a negative thing but as *an opportunity to move our children forward in the right direction.*

- For our younger children (four and younger) conflict can give us the opportunity, by the way we deal with it, to establish in their minds that it's good to do as Mum and Dad say.
- For our older children we can use inappropriate behaviour as an opportunity to help them to understand that what they are doing is an indication of what is going on in their hearts and that what will help is a change of heart.

A good safety valve

Once our children have grasped the need for doing as Mum and Dad say (probably around the age of five), it is a good idea to teach them that it is fine to ask us to think again. This is a good thing because. . .

a) We may have spoken in a hurry without thinking about what we were saying. It allows us to change our mind about something which in retrospect is inappropriate.

b) It protects our children from feeling that they are always in a no-win situation. To know that Mum and Dad will listen to them and reconsider what we have said if necessary and appropriate is a good safety valve.

Helpful responses from our children

a)   On hearing us call they begin to act straight away.
b)   They ask us to rethink respectfully and not in a whine.
c)   They accept graciously that Mum and Dad have the final word.

3. How this works out with very young children

- Set limits and boundaries right from the start. In other words don't give your infant freedoms which you may later regret.
- Don't be afraid to say 'no' to your infant.
- Deal wisely with tantrums.

Our aim is not to focus on behaviour, but rather to see behaviour as an indication of what is going on in our children's hearts.

**A willingness to do as Mum and Dad ask demonstrates
a heart that wants to do the right thing**

Taking it further

1. Spend some time working on having your child do as you ask, putting into practice some of the suggestions from this session.
2. If you have younger children, try making a game out of having your child come to you when he is called with a 'yes Mum' or 'yes Dad'.
3. Try giving a five-minute warning before giving instructions and see how it makes a difference to your child's response.
4. Read Chapter 7 of *Parenting Children.*

8

Taking Corrective Action

Our children will need us to be positive and encouraging as well as corrective if we are to reach their hearts and not frustrate them

---

Our aim is to use discipline as a whole in order to reach the point where our children know what is right and desire to do it because it is the right thing.

1. Life-skills

How can we encourage our child to learn a life-skill?

Praise

Incentives

2. Behaviour

Encouragement

With forethought we can encourage them by giving them prior preparation so that they have every opportunity of doing the right thing.

Work out your family 'Golden Rules' for when you're away from home and have the children see how many things they can remember before arriving at your destination.

For example, at a friend's house

- say hello when they arrive
- take shoes off at the door
- say please and thank you
- don't charge around the house
- ask before playing with toys
- look at adults when speaking to them

Correction

'No discipline seems pleasant at the time, but painful. Later on, however, it produces a harvest of righteousness and peace for those who have been trained by it' (Hebrews 12:11).

Correction is an integral part of discipline. There will be times when it hurts us very much to correct our children and we may be tempted to let things pass. But in the long run our children will miss out if we try to avoid correction just to make life easier for ourselves.

It is a loving parent who seeks to discipline his child wisely and thoughtfully

---

'Let your **gentleness** be evident to all . . .' (Philippians 4:5). If we can approach correction with this in mind, we can't go far wrong!

So how do we know whether or not to correct? Their behaviour could be due to

a) childish innocence
b) childish thoughtlessness
c) deliberate naughtiness

We need to ask ourselves the following questions:

- Are the circumstances hindering my child from doing the right thing?
- Is she particularly tired, or hungry?
- Is he acting out of character or is this something that often occurs and really needs dealing with?
- Is she unwell or is she sickening for something?
- Does he need to go to the toilet?

Deliberate naughtiness can occur on three levels as follows (although this is only a guide and things are rarely black or white!):

a) Small incidents that need a telling off.
b) Naughtiness that needs more than just a verbal telling off:

   - behaviour that occurs frequently
   - warnings that have been ignored
   - past habits that seem to be growing more regular again, e.g. whining. How can we cope with whining?

     - Point out that it is becoming a habit and that it is not an acceptable means of communicating.
     - For a toddler it is often helpful just to say 'no whining' and have them answer you 'Yes Mummy. No whining.'
     - For a slightly older child, if requests come in a whine suggest your child goes away and has a rethink and comes back and asks properly.

— If whining still persists, a stronger form of correction may be needed.

c) Behaviour that will need stronger action, such as:

- time apart from others
- withdrawal of a privilege
- logical consequences

It's important to stress the need for some correction. If we seek to avoid it, we'll likely be frustrated with our disobedient children. Shaping our children will involve both encouragement and correction

---

If our children know we love them unconditionally they will respond so much more readily to our discipline, be it encouragement or correction.

3. Putting things right

Feeling sorry

Forgiving and forgetting

To say sorry only goes part of the way: it acknowledges a mistake.
To ask for forgiveness demonstrates a change of heart

Mum and Dad say sorry too

Remember how important our example is! Forgiveness works both ways and if we are in the wrong it will be very powerful for our children to hear us say sorry and ask for forgiveness.

Making amends

'Discipline should be the framework and encouragement that a loving parent creates for their child in order to help them gradually learn how to control their behaviour, and develop self-discipline. Discipline should be an enabler: a creative force designed to build maturity and consistency, helping children fit into society without being swamped by it. Discipline should give your children the self-control they need to manage what they do, both now and in the future.' (Steve Chalke)

Taking it further

1. Spend some time thinking and talking about how you feel about the way you discipline your children, and discuss any changes that you want to make.
2. Find an opportunity to encourage your children in learning a life-skill.
3. Start putting into practice the encouragement that will help your children know how to respond on different occasions. Try, for example, giving them instruction on what is expected of them at the supermarket or at a friend's house.
4. Look out for examples of childish innocence and deliberate naughtiness. Is it easy to spot the difference?
5. Read Chapter 8 of *Parenting Children*.

9

Modelling Love and Respect

1. Our children's relationship with God

- Valuing all that God has made.

  - As a family, sponsor a child in a developing country, e.g. through the Toybox Charity.
  - Raise money for a project that helps the homeless.
  - Give clothes and toys to others more needy than ourselves.
  - At Christmas take part in a project that gives toys to children who otherwise would not have any, e.g. The Samaritan's Purse.

- Loving God also means remembering that the gifts we have come from him, whether those be musical or sporting or creative gifts or something else.

2. Our children's relationship with Mum and Dad

- Be careful of trying to be friends with your children from day one.

Friendship is our ultimate goal in adulthood and we reach it gradually

- Help your children to respect you by being careful how they speak to you and by correcting them if they are rude.

Practical ideas

- Have Mum and Dad sit at the head of the table at family meal times.
- Have Mum and Dad sit in the front seats of the car.
- Have younger children ask before taking a drink or a biscuit and before using the telephone.

3. Our children's relationship with their brothers and sisters

- Try referring to your children's siblings as 'your brother' or 'your sister' as a change from calling them by their Christian name.
- Try to notice when one of them is being kind to the other and praise them for it.
- Try to encourage them to be glad when something good happens to one of their siblings and praise them when they manage it!
- Squabbles between brothers and sisters are inevitable but needn't get out of hand. Encourage your children to be sensitive to one another's feelings. Teach them how to listen and respond to one another in a way that will build one another up.
- Encourage your children to be aware of the good qualities that their brothers and sisters have.

Children who are fortunate enough to have brothers and sisters have a wonderful opportunity for learning how to put others first and allowing them to feel valued.

4. Our children's relationship with other adults

- Devise some family guidelines about what to do when an adult speaks to them.
- Teach your children how to get your attention in an appropriate way when you are in conversation with another adult.
- Encourage your children from an early age to write thank-you letters for the presents they receive, as a means of demonstrating a sense of the preciousness of others.
- When you go to a public place such as a library or doctor's surgery or certain church services where people particularly need peace and quiet, remind them of that before you arrive.
- Mealtimes are always a great opportunity for thinking of others. Encourage your children to use good manners by not starting until everyone is served, saying 'please' and 'thank you', eating with their lips together and complimenting the cook. These are ways of showing they are thinking of those at the table, guests and family alike.

Even the babies can use good manners. You could teach your baby sign language so that they can say 'please' and 'thank you' and 'more please' and 'drink please' before they can speak (babies can often pick this up from about a year, sometimes earlier). It makes for much more peaceful family mealtimes!

5. Our children's relationship with their friends

- Help them to be glad when something good happens to one of their friends.
- Encourage them to respect their friends' belongings and at other people's houses wait until they are invited to play with the toys before

they dive in. Teach them to understand the value of belongings and property by encouraging them to do little jobs to earn money:

- tidying up the garden of litter
- Dusting and polishing
- Cleaning the windows

- Encourage them to look out for people who might be on their own in the playground and include them in their games.
- To the moan of 'It's not fair', explain to them that life isn't always fair and help them to remember and be thankful for what they have.
- Encourage them to pray for their friends and not just generally but for specific needs.
- Encourage them to feel very privileged when they receive an invitation to a party. Remind them what a privilege it is to be counted as some-one's friend.

Ideas:

- Encourage them to make their own birthday card to give.
- Let them choose and wrap the present with you.
- Have them pay a bit towards the present when they are old enough.

In the early years our children learn more from copying what we do than we realise!

Taking it further

1. When you spot your child being kind to a sibling or friend without being prompted, give him or her lots of praise.
2. Teach your child how to get your attention when you are talking to another person. See how long it takes for them to catch on.
3. Read Chapter 9 of *Parenting Children*.

10
Keeping the Vision in Mind

1. Faith

Have faith in God.

Have faith in your marriage.

Invest in your marriage

- Take time for each other.
- Look for the best in each other.
- Stand together with a mutual sense of values and a common objective.
- Speak words of appreciation.
- Find things to praise in each other.
- Do your best to forgive and forget.
- Don't be an historical partner – that is, one who always digs up the past because you can bury a marriage with a lot of little digs.
- Look to the future, think how you would like it to be and then go for it.

Remember . . . it's not just about marrying the right partner but about being the right partner

---

Have faith in yourself as a parent.

Have faith in your values.

Have faith in your methods of discipline.

Have faith that God has heard your prayers for your children.

2. Hope

Hope is an integral part of being a parent. For Christians, hope brings great strength because it is grounded in the promises of God who helps us through the hardest of times and with whom there is always a brighter future ahead.

- We hope that our children have caught our values.
- We hope that they will have found a passion in life.
- We hope that when our children are small we have instilled in them a sense of purpose, a thirst to make the best of everything and a desire to make a difference in this world.

3. Love

- A love that is accepting and yet guiding.

- A love that does not demand performance and always offers forgiveness.
- A love that seeks to build up and guide in right ways.
- A love that is not afraid to discipline for a better end.

Creating a family vision statement

A vision statement gives you a point of reference as a family. You can look at it and ask yourselves

- How are we doing as a family?
- Are we living out the things we consider to be important?
- Are we spending time together?
- How are we treating each other?
- Are we being encouraging?
- Are we giving as well as taking?
- Are we thinking of those outside the family as well as ourselves?
- Is our home a place of peace and harmony, a place where we all enjoy coming back to?
- Are we living as God would have us live?

Step 1

Either at Family Time or round the family meal table introduce the idea of having a family vision statement. Explain what it is and see what people think of the idea. Say it could include such things as:

- What kind of family do we want to be?
- What kind of atmosphere do we want in our home?
- How do we want to treat each other and speak to one another?
- What are the responsibilities of each family member?
- What things are important to us as a family?

- What guidelines do we want to live by?
- How do we want to treat other people?
- What is the purpose of our family?
- How can we make a difference to the community we live in?

Step 2

Revisit your vision statement together. Go round the family and take turns to say the things that are important. Discuss them as you go, and write them down.

You will need some ground rules:

- Everyone respects what others say.
- Everyone has a chance to say everything they want to.

Step 3

Once everyone is happy with the vision statement, create the final document, have everyone sign it and date it and then display it in the place where you most often gather as a family and use it to keep your destination in mind.

Step 4

Review your vision statement each year.

Here is an example of a vision statement created by one family who followed the *Parenting Children* course (reproduced with permission):

Things that are important to our family

1 All of us are to tell the truth.
2 Do as Mum and Dad say.
3 Mum and Dad are not to aggravate the children.
4 Stealing is always wrong. When we borrow things, we will look after them as if they were our own and not be jealous.
5 We will support and encourage each other, especially when we get things wrong.
6 We will listen to each other.
7 We will show kindness to each other by sharing our own things and time, e.g. by helping around the house.
8 Remember: people are more important than things.
9 It's important to have fun and laughter together as a family.
10 We love God and want to serve him.

Notes

Chapter 3

Fig 1: Ted Tripp, *Shepherding a Child's Heart* (Shepherd Press, 1995).

Chapter 6

How to score the healthy conscience test

91–120	Excessively unhealthy conscience
73–90	Seriously unhealthy conscience
54–72	Highly unhealthy conscience
41–53	Slightly unhealthy conscience
29–40	Healthy conscience
12–28	Possibly a hardened conscience!

Chapter 9

- The Toybox Charity (helping street children in Guatemala and Bolivia) is contactable at: PO Box 660, Amersham, Bucks HP6 6EA. www.toybox.org
- The Samaritan's Purse (working with children in the Eastern Bloc and elsewhere) is contactable at: Samaritans Purse Int. Ltd, Victoria House, Victoria Road, Buckhurst Hill, Essex IG9 5EX.